D0571731

Thrift
⮞ and ⮜
Generosity

The Joy of Giving

That your life may abound
in the joy of John Wesley:

"Make all you can,
Save all you can,
Give all you can—
For as long as you can."

John Templeton Jr.

Thrift
and
Generosity

The Joy of Giving

JOHN M. TEMPLETON JR., MD

FOREWORD BY MILLARD FULLER

Templeton Foundation Press
Philadelphia & London

Templeton Foundation Press
300 Conshohocken State Road, Suite 550
West Conshohocken, Pennsylvania 19428
www.templetonpress.org

Library of Congress Cataloging-in-Publication Data
Templeton, John Marks, 1940-
Thrift and generosity : the joy of giving / John M. Templeton, Jr.
p.   cm.
Includes bibliographical references.
ISBN 1-932031-71-5 (hardcover : alk. paper)
1. Christian giving. 2. Generosity—Religious aspects—Christianity.
3. Saving and investment. I. Title.
BV772.T435 2004
179'.9—dc22   2004011002

Designed and typeset by Helene Krasney
Printed in the United States of America

09   10   11   12   13   10 9 8 7 6 5 4 3 2

I wish to express my deepest gratitude and appreciation to Mr. Randy Frame, Dr. Arthur Schwartz, and to Rev. Dr. Peter Lillback for their invaluable assistance.

· CONTENTS ·

· FOREWORD ·

What a great little book! You are in for a treat as you read this superb publication on two subjects—thrift and generosity—that should be of vital concern and interest to every person.

This is the first time I've ever read something that puts thrift and generosity together and explains so beautifully their natural connection.

Thrift is clearly a virtue. Dr. Templeton makes that point plainly and convincingly in the following pages. I resonate strongly with what he writes about thrift because I consider myself a thrifty person. Waste of any kind is abhorrent to me.

On the other hand, being generous and sharing with others fills me with joy. And, Dr. Templeton writes so beautifully about the joy that generosity brings to the life of any person.

You are about to be enlightened and enriched as you read this magnificent essay. The experience you are about to have should make you more thrifty and more generous. And that should make you a better and more joyous person. Keep reading and don't stop until you've read every word. You'll be glad you did!

> Millard Fuller
> Founder and President
> Habitat for Humanity International

· THRIFT AND GENEROSITY ·

· INTRODUCTION ·

Human beings are united, among other things, by a common striving for happiness. Everyone wants to be happy. In the Declaration of Independence, Thomas Jefferson specifically cites the universal goals of life, liberty, and the pursuit of happiness. We pursue happiness in different ways. Though they may not find it there, some pursue happiness by accumulating material things. Some emphasize building close relationships, while others seek happiness in their vocation or through certain activities or hobbies. But we all want happiness. Most would agree there is something missing—something wrong, something fractured—in the person who claims that happiness is not important to him or to her.

My hope for this book, however, is both to challenge and to enable readers to strive for something even more significant, something even greater than happiness. That something is joy. To be sure, happiness and joy are similar concepts. They are related emotions. They bring to mind similar states of mind or being. In fact, I can appreciate that some would see no difference between the two.

To my way of thinking, however, happiness and joy are not the same. Both, of course, carry positive connotations. But when I think of happiness, I think of a state that in some way is tied to circumstances. I think of a state of being or feeling that to some extent exists at the surface of our lives, something transient, changeable. Happiness is real, but potentially impermanent. It is influenced by prevailing conditions.

Joy, in contrast, suggests something deeper, more lasting. Joy implies a state of mind or being that dwells in the depths of the soul. It implies a degree of contentment too strong and secure to be influenced by the changing circumstances of our lives. Negative developments may deprive a person of outward happiness, but nothing can take away that person's inner joy.

In our quest for joy, we will focus in particular on two important virtues: thrift and generosity. Both of these virtues (but especially thrift) have to some extent been forgotten in modern times—or at least greatly underappreciated as virtues.

Each of these qualities—thrift and generosity—is a virtue in its own right. This is to say, there is great merit in practicing thrift, even if it is practiced independently of other virtues. The same is true of generosity. In these pages, we will examine various aspects of both thrift and generosity, including the relationship between practicing these virtues and the striving toward spiritual maturity.

My hope, however, is that this book will make a unique contribution as a result of its focus on practicing these virtues in concert with one another. The direction of this book is well summarized by these words from the founder of Methodism, John Wesley: "Make all you can, save all you can, give all you can." Through his prolific writings and speaking engagements, Wesley earned a small fortune over his lifetime. Nevertheless, he was continually giving to others in ways that he felt would build the Kingdom. At the end of his life, his physical possessions included just one well-worn coat and two silver spoons.

I believe that as much as either thrift or generosity has to offer independently, they offer far, far more when practiced together. Indeed, my hope is that we will discover that the whole that results from practicing these virtues in tandem will greatly exceed the sum of the parts. And I am further convinced that this line of thinking will move us closer to the goal of discovering and experiencing true joy.

· THRIFT ·

I n a game of word association, many, upon hearing the word "thrifty," are likely to respond with such words as "cheap" and "cheapskate." After all, "thrifty" and "cheap" are similar in meaning. Both words, for example, suggest a conservative approach to money: spending less—getting by with less—even when it is possible to spend more. A periodical whose purpose is to encourage debt-proof living (i.e., thrift) is entitled *The Cheapskate Monthly*.

Despite their similarity in meaning, however, the idiom of our culture makes a clear distinction between "thrifty" and "cheap." The two words carry markedly different connotations. Though we may not be immediately able to pinpoint why, we tend to think positively of a person who is described as being thrifty, while negative thoughts come to mind upon hearing about someone who is cheap. No one, for example, is likely to consider Dickens's Mr. Scrooge as being thrifty. On the other hand, Scrooge, prior to his transformation, is the ultimate cheapskate. To put it simply, thrift is good, especially when it is coupled with some greater purpose; but cheap is bad, especially when the focus is on self and not on others.

An Ancient Parable

Understanding the differences between "thrifty" and "cheap," subtle though they may be, will go a long way toward uncovering the full meaning and significance of thrift. Jesus' Parable of the Talents, as recorded in the New Testament Gospel of Matthew, helps to zero in on these differences.

The parable begins with a man who is going on a journey. He chooses three servants to look after his resources, or in other words, his talents (a talent being a unit of currency), while he is gone. He entrusts the first servant with five talents. The second servant receives two, while the third gets only one.

As soon as their master leaves town, the first servant goes to work, putting the talents to good use. In fact, by the time the boss returns, the first servant has turned the five talents he was given into ten. The second servant was able to achieve similar success, despite less "start-up cash." He was able to convert the two talents he was given into four. Their master, needless to say, is very pleased with the first two servants, because they exhibited one of the hallmarks of thrift—namely, being a true steward of the assets in one's care.

He is not so pleased with servant number three, who was guided not by stewardship but by fear and lethargy. In fact, the third servant did nothing with the one talent he had been given beyond digging a hole in the ground and burying it for safekeeping. The master punishes the third servant by taking the only talent he has and giving it the servant who had ten.

Opportunity is missed by most people

because it is dressed in overalls

and looks like work.

—THOMAS EDISON

Upon hearing this story for the first time, many people find the conclusion a bit jarring. By and large, the traditional teachings of the world's major religions, including Christianity, promote compassion and mercy for the poor. We are not accustomed to seeing the person who was given the least with which to work being judged so harshly in the end. The message of the Parable of the Talents, however, does not conflict with the biblical theme of God's concern for the poor and powerless. Its message focuses not on what we have been given—whether it is five talents, two, one, ten, or more. It focuses rather on what we *do* with what we have been given, whether the gift was a little or a lot.

As I previously indicated, there may be some similarities between "thrifty" and "cheap," such as in the aphorism "waste not, want not." However, this parable makes a clear distinction between the two concepts. The servant who received five talents and the one who received two were thrifty. We can presume that they were industrious, hard working, and probably even creative in their handling of their master's resources. In contrast, the servant who received one talent was cheap. He had no ambition and was unwilling to take even a slight risk. He was, in all likelihood, lazy.

The Parable of the Talents points toward a meaning of "thrift" that goes far beyond a kind of inertia of simply spending less or doing less. Again, the third servant spent nothing and did nothing, yet he can in no way be considered thrifty. Let us explore some of the other qualities that distinguish thriftiness from merely being cheap.

Thrift and Human Industry

Genuine thrift is rooted in the philosophical understanding that life is a gift to be explored and enjoyed. All we have to do is look around us each day to recognize that the people we work with and live among represent a variety of talents and abilities, as well as different levels of talent, ability, and resources. Some

may have unusual athletic ability. Others may have keen powers of intellect or they may be dancers or musicians. Some have unique communication skills, while others have the gift of patience, understanding, or empathy.

People who keep their gifts to themselves may be cheap, but they are not thrifty. Those who spend most of their time at home being entertained by mindless television, who have no desire to explore the world around them, who do not care to get to know people who may be different from them, who do nothing with their financial resources except what it takes to be comfortable, are very likely to be cheap. But they cannot be considered thrifty.

Thrifty people are those who are out in the world living life, not just enduring it. Thrifty people are stewards of their talents by learning a new language or exploring a better way of doing business. They are sending spaceships to Mars to learn more about the physical universe and they are exploring

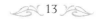

I recommend you to holy simplicity.

—FRANCIS DE SALES

new dimensions of human spirituality. They are taking piano lessons, learning a new sport, going to the opera, finding creative ways to reach and teach inner-city children who come from broken or troubled homes, developing more effective medical technology. They are investing their financial resources responsibly in potentially profitable ventures. Sometimes this entails taking a risk that they will lose part of what they have. But they are not content to bury what they have in the ground.

Thrifty people do not shy away from a hard day's work. They recognize the relationship between sacrifice and reward. They do not expect to get something for nothing.

Instead of going into hiding, thrifty people are out there in the world exercising their gifts and using their resources—working, thinking, creating—making the most of what they have been given, following the example of the first two servants in the Parable of the Talents.

I can recall a television commercial from several years ago that featured an elderly man who was obviously very wealthy. He had to decide between the more expensive product and the less expensive one that, presumably, could do the same job. He chose the less expensive option, prompting a bystander to pose the question, "Why would a man like him care about which item costs less?" The wealthy man's limousine driver responded, "My friend, how do you think a man like him got to be a man like him?"

Thrift, in a way that "cheap" does not, implies an element of human wisdom, of discernment. For example, if you choose a less expensive item that fits your need, then you will have more resources for some other need. We can presume that the first two servants in the Parable of the Talents did not throw their money at the first opportunity that came along. Otherwise, assuming human nature back then was what it is today, they would likely have lost it. As we well know, there are plenty of ruthless advertisers and businesspersons around today who are willing, ready, and able to take full advantage of people who act before they think.

From time to time we hear of celebrities—whether athletes or musicians or actors—who once had all the financial resources they could ever need but lost everything through wasteful spending or bad investments. Thrifty people are discerning people. A thrifty person does not just consider the cheapest price, but the value—the reliability, the effectiveness—of the object he or she is purchasing or the entity in which he or she is investing. A battery that costs twice as much as another battery is worth the price if it lasts three times as long.

In considering how they will use their resources, thrifty people are committed to making careful, thoughtful decisions. This does not make them cheap; it makes them wise.

*Stop trying to impress people
with your clothes and impress them
with your life.*

—RICHARD FOSTER

A Culture of Wastefulness

In the February 6, 2004, issue of the *Philadelphia Inquirer,* columnist Tom Ferrick Jr. tells the story of Neil Benson, who has fashioned a career out of being a "dumpster diver." Benson and a few dozen associates regularly go through garbage to find things that have been trashed before their time. Benson has made children's toys out of old lamps, earrings out of typewriter keys, and jewelry boxes from license plates.

Benson is quoted as saying, "I believe trash is simply a failure of imagination." Benson views his work as an antidote to what he considers America's criminal culture of wastefulness. "This country throws out more," he says, "than other countries make."

Even those who are not called to a career in dumpster diving would do well to note the truth that motivates Neil Benson and his cohorts. Wastefulness is a by-product of a materialistic culture bent on producing more and more things, often without sufficiently considering whether all the things are needed or even wanted. Toys routinely tossed away after the garage sale ends would be the envy of many a child in a developing country.

A life of thrift entails saying no to things we do not truly need. It also entails draining every ounce of usefulness out of the things we do acquire before throwing them away, an approach that would free Neil Benson up to pursue a different career.

Many people with limited incomes have learned to be thrifty out of necessity. But one need not be poor to be thrifty, as evidenced by a story in the *Wall Street Journal* featuring Warren Buffet, one of the world's wealthiest people. A photo accompanying the article showed the famed investment guru standing by his brand new car. It was a Lincoln Town Car. Buffet is obviously not cheap. But the article pointed out that this was his first new car in ten years. Prominent in the photo was the license plate, which read THRIFTY.

When it came to buying a new car, Mr. Buffet bought the best, or one of the best. But, unlike those who think they need a new car every year or two, he is apparently intent on getting his money's worth. No doubt his commitment to thrift—to making use of something until its usefulness is used up—comes through in other areas of his life as well. Thrifty people are not wasteful people.

The virtue of thrift is essential if we are to preserve our natural environment for future generations. In this regard, we in the United States have much to learn from some of those who lived here before us. In *Living More with Less*, Doris Janzen Longacre informs us that the Wintu Indians of California "burned only dead wood for fuel and used every portion of a hunted animal's carcass." They had a deep reverence for the gifts of the earth, taking nothing for granted.

On many fronts, we have made a lot of progress in improving our environment over the last few decades. But much

The virtue of gratitude . . .
directly touches the ultimate foundations
of human existence, for there is hardly
another quality of man that is so suited
to reveal the state of his inner spiritual
and moral health as his capacity to be grateful.

—OTTO FRIEDRICH BOLLNOW

remains to be done. I recognize that there are different perspectives in the scientific community as to what warrants the greatest attention regarding the environment. Objective science rather than ideology should always be our guide. But we should all be able to unite behind the biblical principle that we are stewards, not owners, of the resources with which God has blessed us. With this perspective as a part of our worldview, we should all be motivated by the virtue of thrift.

THRIFT AND GRATITUDE

The commitment to getting the most out of the things we have begins with a grateful attitude. I believe there is a direct correlation between wastefulness and a lack of gratitude for the things we are fortunate enough to possess. After all, it only makes sense that if someone is truly grateful, truly appreciates what he or she has been given, the person will take good care of it. Whether a child with a common toy or a wealthy businessman with a yacht, those who are grateful will be good stewards of their possessions. They will get the longest life and the most use out of the things for which they are truly thankful. In fact, as true stewards, they will continually be mindful of the value of things that they have and how these things can be used to benefit others.

THRIFT AND ETHICAL STANDARDS

A friend once took a car to a mechanic who was able to find several things wrong with it in addition to the original problem. To fix it all would cost about $700. He went to a second mechanic, who said that a lot of what the first mechanic was recommending was not really necessary, at least not right away. The second mechanic said he could have the car up and running for less than $200, and if the other problems occurred down the line, he would address them then.

Not surprisingly, my friend chose car mechanic number two. This mechanic settled for under $200, when he probably could have gotten another $300 or $400 out of his customer. But his honesty and commitment to looking out for what was best for his client earned him a customer for life. What he lost on that first day, he more than made up for in the months and years to come.

This commitment to integrity is something my father, Sir John Templeton, realized early on. One of the secrets to his remarkable success as a businessman and investment manager was his recognition of the relationship between thrift and ethics. He was convinced that one of the most important components of success in business was the practice of high ethical standards. He observed that those who prospered in business in the long run were those who put service and concern for others at the top of their list of priorities.

While some people may gain a temporary economic advantage by cutting corners or even by taking advantage of others, my father realized that, over time, unless you treat your customer better than your competitor does, the customer will eventually

Sloth, like rust, consumes faster than labour wears,
while the used key is always bright.
Want of care does more damage
than want of knowledge.
Beware of little expenses;
a small leak will sink a great ship.
A ploughman on his legs is higher
than a gentleman on his knees.
Always taking out of the pot, and never putting in,
one soon comes to the bottom.
It is hard for an empty bag to stand upright.

—Benjamin Franklin

go to the competitor. And unless you and your enterprise build a reputation for reliability and honesty, your customers will one day turn to others who may more faithfully value their interests. One of the best ways to be thrifty in business is to be ethical.

Thrift and Discipline

A thrifty life is a disciplined life. One of the distinguishing marks of contemporary U.S. culture is the inability of individuals and families (and many organizations, for that matter) to live within their means. In the end, if there are not sufficient controls and limits on what a family or a business is spending, it does not matter how much the family or the business is earning. The result of overspending will be the steady, erosive impact of debt.

Many have the requisite discipline to earn a sufficient income but lack the discipline required to keep from spending it all and then some. As a culture, we are inundated with a seemingly limitless number of gizmos and gadgets—from better phones and bigger televisions to climate-controlled cars and nose-hair trimmers—to make our lives easier, more convenient and comfortable. We are not content with the amenities of a previous generation that, in fact, have often served our needs very well. In our zeal for new things—just because they are new—we often do not ask the "value" of what we are purchasing. Without asking this question, we often end up in more debt.

In his timeless masterpiece *Poor Richard's Almanac,* Benjamin Franklin often spoke about debt in a variety of contexts: "Never to go into debt; or, if accident should render a trifling debt necessary; to have at home more than enough to defray it." "If you would know the value of money, go and try to borrow some, for he that goes a borrowing goes a sorrowing." And lastly, "Think what you do when you run in debt; you give to another power over your liberty."

For the record, there is nothing inherently wrong with any product or service intended to make life more interesting or more enjoyable or comfortable. But it *is* a problem when people are not able to say no to the things they impulsively want or think they need but clearly cannot afford. An inability to live within our means is the exact opposite of a life of thrift.

This lack of financial discipline is reflected by our culture of debt. In addition to the home mortgage, car loans, and loans for appliances and home improvements, the typical American household carries nearly $6,000 in credit card debt, usually at interest rates in the high teens.

In his 2001 book *Affluenza: The All Consuming Epidemic,* John DeGraaf gave a name to our culture's obsession with wanting more. Fortunately, the disease of "affluenza" has an antidote. That antidote is a life of discipline. By and large, there are no great secrets or mysteries surrounding a life of discipline. Simple common sense should inform us that no individual, family, or

No person will occasion to complain
of the want of time who never loses any.

—THOMAS JEFFERSON

business operation can avoid ultimate crisis if monthly expenses exceed monthly income on a regular basis. Sometimes a life of discipline entails making an effort to distinguish between genuine needs and mere wants, and then simply saying no to the latter.

Even those who agree in principle with the simple logic of this approach may have trouble following it. We've all heard it more than a few times: "I don't know where all the money goes!" The solution to this frustrating reality is to find out where all the money goes by keeping a list of all expenses—cash, check, and credit card—for at least a month, but preferably for two or three. Many who have tried this exercise have found out that the occasional splurge on nonessential items or services was not so occasional after all. Seeing the evidence on paper enabled them to become more disciplined spenders.

Thrift and Tithing

As we will see later, many world religions teach some version of the principle of tithing or giving away a designated portion of income to support religious and charitable causes. In my Christian tradition, that percentage is one-tenth.

Many are hesitant to give away one-tenth of their income because they feel they cannot afford it. Such persons should know, however, that a very high percentage of people who have given tithing a chance usually stay with it because they believe they cannot afford to stop tithing. Gordon Groth, former president of Electra Manufacturing Co., once observed that he knew plenty of people who stopped going to church for one reason or another, but he wasn't aware of anyone who had ever stopped tithing once they had started. In fact, committed tithers almost universally indicate that they wish they had started sooner.

Many have experienced how tithing has a powerful spiritual and even material impact on one's life. One reason is that those who make a commitment to tithe are forced to establish a financial discipline. In creating your budget for the year, if you put your tithe at the top of your budget, a natural sense of the true priorities for the rest of your budget will soon become clear. Once this sort of discipline occurs, it extends its influence to all other areas of your financial picture.

Beyond the material benefits, many credit tithing with bringing to their lives an element of joy and contentment that was not there previously, but I will save this discussion for the final section.

Thrift and Hard Work

An Italian immigrant who found success in the United States wanted to help newer immigrants get started in this country. The wealthy man wanted to provide loans, but he wanted to make sure his generosity would be employed wisely. Most of the new arrivals applying for loans had no collateral to offer: no house or other possessions. So the banker asked to take a look at the applicants' hands. He was looking for calluses, and if he found them, he considered them collateral. A callus to him was a sign that a person was not afraid of a hard day's work. He

Buy what thou hast no need of,
and ere long thou shalt sell thy necessaries.

—BENJAMIN FRANKLIN

knew that a major part of America's success was achieved by people who were not afraid of hard work, and that opportunities for success and even prosperity usually followed from hard work. This brings to mind more of Benjamin Franklin's wisdom in *Poor Richard's Almanac:* "There are no gains without pains" and "Diligence is the mother of good luck."

As established by the Parable of the Talents, thrift encompasses far more than simply not spending. It entails being willing to put whatever talents, skills, and abilities we may have to work. Philosopher Kahlil Gibran best expressed the spiritual dimension of work: "Work is love made visible." To be sure, there is a need to balance work with the human needs—and wants—of our families and loved ones for a portion of our time. Nevertheless, there are still plenty of people around who are living examples of the maxim "Idleness is the thief of time."

The legendary Alabama football coach Bear Bryant is reported to have said, "Football is 50,000 people who desperately need exercise watching 22 people who desperately need rest." Similarly, there are many in our society who have become workaholics, who are under great stress, who need to experience the rejuvenating powers of some good old-fashioned R & R. Others, however, are challenged to realize that it's just as easy to waste time as it is to waste money.

Just as keeping track of expenditures can be revealing, so can keeping track of how your time is spent. Those who record for a month or two how they spend their time might be surprised to learn how many hours they spend in front of the television or playing computer games and how little time they spend talking with family and friends or serving as volunteers for the betterment of society.

Thrift and Gambling

Thrift recognizes a relationship between immediate sacrifice and ultimate gain, between hard work and high reward. That such values have largely gone into seclusion in our culture is evidenced by the growing acceptance of gambling. In essence, gambling attracts and exploits people who want something for nothing, who desire rewards without being willing to make the appropriate sacrifices.

Programs—even whole societies—built on such values cannot succeed for long. For this reason, those who support a culture of thrift would do well to oppose the efforts by governments at various levels to raise revenues through "gaming," an all-too-obvious euphemism, since there is nothing inherently uplifting about rolling dice or spinning a wheel.

Studies have established a clear, positive correlation between gambling and budgetary problems at the state level. In 2003, Nevada Governor Kenny Guinn complained to the Nevada legislature: "My fellow Nevadans, the lessons from the past twenty years is clear; our revenue (system) is broken because it has relied on regressive and unstable gambling taxes." Meanwhile in neighboring Utah, Governor Mike Leavitt attributed his state's

*There's as much risk in doing nothing
as in doing something.*

−TRAMMELL CROW

success at job creation and personal income growth directly to his state's "no gaming" status.

Every dollar put into a slot machine is a dollar that could have been spent supporting local businesses that make a clear and measurable, positive contribution to society. In addition, as John Warren Kindt, a professor at the University of Illinois at Urbana-Champaign who has studied the gambling industry and testified at Congressional hearings, points out, "there is no such thing as 'limited gambling.' Since gambling creates no product, it must continue to expand into more gambling types and jurisdictions, draining increasing amounts of consumer dollars from pre-existing businesses." And we have not even mentioned the correlation between gambling and such social pathologies as family breakup, domestic abuse and neglect, bankruptcy, embezzlement, suicide, and political corruption.

Lose an hour in the morning and
you will spend all day looking for it

—Richard Whatley

Again, thrift is not so much a matter of how much we have, but of how much we appreciate, value, and use what we have. Everyone, regardless of income level, has opportunities to exercise the virtue of thrift. We practice thrift by monitoring how we spend our time and money and then by making better decisions.

Sometimes being thrifty entails being less concerned about public image. It may mean forming a dinner group and eating at home instead of going out to high-priced restaurants. It can mean buying clothes at a thrift shop or making a Christmas or birthday gift for a friend or family member instead of buying one. Alternatively, one might choose an inexpensive vacation that puts you in touch with another culture instead of spending lots of money at a tourist trap.

Publications such as *The Cheapskate Monthly* and the aptly titled book *Living More with Less* provide many more ideas for making thrift a higher priority. Remember that thrift means far more than being cheap. It is not simply a matter of under-standing the "bottom line." Thrift, rather, is part of a spiritual and cultural understanding of how we use our time, our talents, and our resources. Creating a culture of thrift means embedding this virtue in a larger framework of personal responsibility, dis-cipline, purpose, and future-mindedness. To the extent that the virtue of thrift has been forgotten, it is time to remember it again.

· GENEROSITY ·

All of the world's great religions promote the concept that we live not just for ourselves, but for others. The Torah states: "Deeds of giving are the very foundation of the world." It further commands: "There shall be no needy among you" and "Thou shalt love thy neighbor as thyself."

When a rich young man asked Jesus what he needed to do to achieve perfection, Jesus replied, "Go sell your possessions and give to the poor, and you will have treasure in heaven." This is just one of many admonitions to generosity to be found in the Christian Scriptures and throughout Christian history.

Within the Baha'i faith community, there exists the concept of Huquq'u'llah, or the Right of God, something akin to a tithe

A bit of fragrance always clings
to the hand that gives you roses.

—CHINESE PROVERB

———— • ————

Live and let live is not enough.
Live and help live is not too much.

—ORION E. MADISON

on wealth amounting to 19 percent of net income after expenses. This tithe is to be given to a common fund to advance the faith and its charitable activities.

Buddhists place a special emphasis on self-help and avoiding debt to counter economic difficulties. In line with this notion of thrift, the Buddhist faith community engages in many philanthropic activities such as the Rahula Trust, whose purpose is to help young and disadvantaged children who live in impoverished countries around the world.

Strong support for the relief of poverty can be found within the Hindu faith community. This is evidenced in part by their support for Sewa International, a Hindu aid society. (*Sewa* is an ancient word meaning "service.") It specifically supports such programs as free basic education for all as a way to raise the standard of living, especially among women. In fact, the foundation for all Hindu ethical thought consists of the three *Das:* restraint (self-control), giving, and compassion.

For Muslims, charity (the giving of alms) is the third of the five pillars of Islam. The Islamic concept of almsgiving entails an annual payment of at least 2.5 percent of one's wealth—not just income, but total assets. The Islamic perspective on generosity is that the rich are responsible for care of the poor so that all of humanity can achieve a common bond, sharing one another's happiness and sorrows.

The collective body of religious thought in this area is overwhelming. So deeply is the concept of generosity intertwined with religious faith that one could argue that any "religious teaching" that denies the virtue of generosity does not belong in the category of a religious teaching that might claim universality.

The gifts we have been given—whether material, intellectual, or artistic—are ours to enjoy, but they are also ours to share. We are part of a larger community. There is a sense in which the whole world is one big community. We need other cultures and other people—and others need us—in order to live and learn to our fullest potential. Sometimes we are in a position of need. Oftentimes those who are fortunate to live in the wealthiest of nations are in a position to give. The challenge for us is to be stewards in our giving—to give in a way that empowers and uplifts the recipient so that what we give is not so much a handout as a hand-up. As a test of your giving, you will know that the cycle is complete when you find that the recipient of your gift becomes a giver in turn.

Starting Young

A cartoon in *Parade* magazine features a mother leaving a store with a defeated look on her face. Her daughter is following her, holding a package and sporting a victorious smile. The caption reads, "You know, Mom, for a minute there—when you said, 'For the last time, no!'—I almost thought you meant it."

Another cartoon, this one in *Teacher* magazine, features a student at her teacher's desk on the first day of school saying,

*Deeds of giving are the equivalent
to the entirety of God's commandment.*

—THE TALMUD

•

*Good will come to him who is generous
and lends freely, who conducts
his affairs with justice.*

—PSALM 112:5

"I didn't do anything on my summer vacation—should I write about what I bought?"

In an article in *Science News*, Bruce Bower reports that, according to California psychologist Allen Kanner, until about ten years ago, children being treated for emotional and behavioral problems said they wanted to grow up to be astronauts, doctors, baseball players, or ballerinas. Today most say they just want to be rich. And many of the children, Bower reports, refuse to play with the conventional toys child psychologists have traditionally kept on hand. They demand electronic games or more elaborate toys.

I fear that a high percentage of the children of the current generation are growing up with a sense of entitlement when it comes to material things. Many teens feel cheated and deprived if they don't have their own television sets in their own bedrooms along with their own personal computers, cell phones, and, when they are of age, automobiles (with, of course, the most advanced CD players). Such attitudes compete with the virtue of generosity.

As our children grow, we teach them what they need to survive and thrive in the world. They learn to read, to eat healthy foods, to follow rules. Perhaps they learn to play a musical instrument or a sport. Many parents teach their children how to choose the right schools and make the right connections so that someday they can make lots of money. I am concerned that not enough of our children are learning how to be generous.

In *More Give to Live,* Dr. Douglas Lawson provides evidence that the urge toward generosity begins early in life. He describes a continuum that he calls the "Giving Path." This path begins with parents teaching and modeling examples of generous behavior. When the children are old enough to go to school, the Giving Path continues, with teachers and religious instructors reinforcing principles of generous behavior.

Eventually children begin to give and to share on their own, using their own resources to help those in need. In their teen years, they embark on volunteer service—perhaps a home-building project or spending time with mentally or physically disabled persons. These patterns continue into adulthood. Sharing resources becomes a natural part of a life, a responsibility that is not burdensome, but is rather accepted and even welcomed.

A few years ago at a gathering on National Philanthropy Day, one of the daughters of John D. Rockefeller told of how her father had given her an allowance of fifteen cents a week. She had three boxes. One-third of her allowance (a nickel) she placed in a box labeled MINE. She placed another nickel each week into a box labeled SAVINGS. And the third nickel she placed into a box labeled OTHERS. She indicated that she had continued throughout her life to abide by her father's principle of "one-third to charity."

Billionaire H. Ross Perot is another example of how powerful early models of generosity can be. Even though he came from a

Whoever sows sparingly will also reap sparingly,
and whoever sows generously will also reap generously.
Each man should give what he has decided
in his heart to give, not reluctantly
or under compulsion, for God loves a cheerful giver.
And God is able to make all grace abound to you,
so that in all things at all times,
having all that you need,
you will abound in every good work.

—2 CORINTHIANS 9:6–8

very poor family, he remembers his mother reaching out to those who had even less by feeding hungry people during the Great Depression. Not surprisingly, Mr. Perot became one our nation's most generous philanthropists.

Our children will grow old soon enough; so let's teach them while they are yet young. Perhaps they will not have much to give, but if it represents a sacrifice, it will have meaning. The amount is not important; it's the principle that matters. Once the value of sharing is taught and a pattern is in place, the amounts will surely change. Someone who began as a child giving away nickels and dimes will be much more open in later life to even greater giving—especially when guided by the principle of helping others to help themselves.

More Than One Path

While the "Giving Path" sets forth the ideal, this does not mean that those for whom generosity has not been modeled have no chance to become generous. I believe in the power of conversion.

I believe it is never too late for someone to change. I know people who were once stingy but who became generous because they were moved to action by someone else's need or by a vision of the difference a well-conceived, strategic gift could make.

As adults, we who are trying to become more generous need to seek opportunities to be among those who are less fortunate than ourselves—from a day spent serving at an inner-city soup kitchen to a church-sponsored short-term mission trip to an impoverished country. Such a visit might open our eyes and our minds to the impact that micro-enterprise loans, for example, can make in transforming a community. These experiences can awaken our sensitivities as human beings and put us on a path of greater generosity.

Generosity and Empathy

Among the marks of spiritual maturity is a person's capacity to empathize with others. And there is a clear connection between empathy and a commitment to generosity. It stands to reason that the more we are able to understand and even to feel the needs and hurts of others—their hunger, sadness, sense of confusion, or hopelessness—the more we will desire to put our resources to work to break this cycle and to contribute to a framework that fosters hope and rewards people for their efforts.

When we are children, we often lack the capacity for empathy. Therefore, young children may exhibit a focus on self and not on others. Learning to share is among the first steps toward acknowledging the needs and feelings of others. As we grow older, most of us learn enough about respect for others to get along in society. But for many, the ability to empathize ends there.

Those with the greatest capacity for empathy—the Mother Teresas of the world—we come to regard as saints. On the opposite end of the spectrum are those whose emotional, social, or spiritual development is arrested for some reason. They may have very little ability to empathize. Perhaps their capacity to see life from another's point of view is so limited that they have no

Surplus wealth is a sacred trust which its possessor
is bound to administer in his lifetime
for the good of the community.

—ANDREW CARNEGIE

reservations about cheating other people or stealing from others or perhaps even taking someone's life. While we obviously need laws and a penal system to contain the damage such people can do, we also need a society compassionate enough to help them recover what is missing in their lives. Perhaps our capacity to be generous and forgiving can help other people to uncover their own capacity for generosity.

BEYOND SELFISHNESS

Of course, as we weigh our own needs and desires against the needs and desires of others, we all have perceived limits on what we can give, what we can share with others without compromising our well-being. Those who are striving toward spiritual maturity in the journey through life are engaged in the constant process of stretching those limits. In other words, the spiritually maturing person strives at every point along the way to become less selfish and more generous—with his or her time, talent, and/or resources.

Putting the needs of others ahead of our own needs is rarely if ever easy, at least at first. Some might argue that the resources we have available to give to others are, after all, limited. They would say that the more money we give to others, the less we have to spend on ourselves. The more time and energy we give to others, the less we have available to do the things that, at least on the surface, appear to make life less stressful and more enjoyable.

That giving is a sign of spiritual maturity is evidenced in the biblical account of the widow's mite. Jesus observes the crowd putting money into the temple treasury. Some very wealthy people contribute some very large amounts. But then a poor woman comes forth and puts in two coins, the smallest unit of currency in circulation at the time. Seizing the opportunity to teach, Jesus pronounces, "[T]his poor widow has put more into the treasury than all the others. They all gave out of their wealth; but she, out of her poverty, put in everything—all she had to live on."

Commenting on this Bible passage, Richard Foster, a contemporary writer on Christian spirituality, observes that it follows closely on the heels of Jesus' disclosure of the two Great Commandments, the first of which is to love God with all of one's heart, soul, mind, and strength. Writes Foster, "Here was a woman free from idolatry to mammon, devoid of greed and avarice. Here was a person in whom extravagant giving exceeded prudent thrift." My father, Sir John Templeton, has often said, "The more love you give, the more you have left." He also suggested as a law of life: "Love given grows, love hoarded dwindles."

MODELS OF GENEROSITY

Among the most generous people I have been blessed to know was a stockbroker from Philadelphia named Harry Kuch. Harry was the son of immigrant parents who made their living as bakers. In his teen years, Harry became a committed Christian and launched a career in investments with the goal of serving others.

Command those who are rich
in this present world not to be arrogant
nor to put their hope in wealth, which is so uncertain,
but to put their hope in God, who richly provides us
with everything for our enjoyment.
Command them to do good, to be rich in good deeds,
and to be generous and willing to share.

—1 TIMOTHY 6:17–18

I got to know Harry near the end of his career. He was among the most joyful people I have ever met. And he shared with his clients the secret to his joy. While many display their generosity by leaving a large bequest, Harry advised his clients to experience the impact of their giving while they were still alive. He coined the following phrase: "If you're giving while you're living, then you're knowing where it's going."

Harry organized most of his charitable giving in a way that allowed him to witness its impact, but he did so quietly. His goal was to see the fruits of his gifts, not to draw attention to himself.

Gladys Holm, who died in 1996 at the age of eighty-six, was known at the Children's Memorial Hospital in Chicago as the "Teddy Bear Lady." She was a retired secretary who lived in a modest apartment in nearby Evanston, Illinois. Her modus operandi was to bring teddy bears to sick children, but during her visits, she would find out about the family's needs. If a family had no money, she would pay their medical bills, but she always did so anonymously.

Nobody knew about the stock options she received in 1951, when she went to work as a secretary for Foster McGraw, the founder of American Hospital Supply. In her will, Gladys left $18 million to be used for medical research for diseases of the heart. Her generosity has helped and will continue to help children for many years to come.

Many Americans today do not realize or appreciate the extraordinary sacrifices George Washington made in the establishment of the United States. During his lifetime, his fellow countrymen commonly recognized the indispensable impact of Washington's unbending integrity and his ever-present generosity.

In 1783, Washington wrote to a relative, "Let your heart feel for the afflictions and distresses of everyone, and let your hand give in proportion to your purse." An employee of Washington observed,

He owned several fishing stations on the Potomac, at which excellent herring were caught, and which, when salted, proved an important article of food to the poor. For their accommodation, he appropriated a station— one of the best he had, and furnished it with all the necessary apparatus for taking herring. Here the honest poor might fish free of expense, at any time. . . . By this means, all the poor round about had the means of procuring a complete stock of this valuable food for their families.

Instead of giving the fish as handouts, Washington recognized that the dignity of those in need was best preserved by enabling them to meet their own needs.

These are just three examples of people whose generosity was accompanied by a spirit of great humility. The world's religions consistently teach that the purpose of giving is not for show or earthly recognition. The ancient Spanish rabbi and philosopher Maimonides defined eight levels of charity. The penultimate level

There are those who have little and give it all.
These are the believers in life and the bounty
of life and their coffers are never empty.

—Kahlil Gibran

focused on giving to charitable organizations so that the donor is unaware of who is benefiting and the recipients do not know to whom they are indebted. The mere act of giving—devoid of any desire for acclaim or even thanks—constitutes its own reward, brings its own sense of joy and contentment.

Generosity and Time

Many people instinctively associate generosity with material resources. However, as was the case with thrift, generosity encompasses not just money, but time. In fact, it is often the case that what is needed in a particular situation is something that no amount of money can buy. Think, for example, of the teenage child who has everything he can possibly ask for: his own room, his own television with all the cable channels, his own car, and an ample allowance. But what he may really want is a closer relationship with his father, who, ironically, is too busy making more money so his son can have his own car and television.

Train a child in the way he should go,
and when he is old he will not turn from it. . . .
A generous man will himself be blessed,
for he shares his food with the poor.

—PROVERBS 22:6–9

According to statistics published by the *Chronicle of Philanthropy,* the roots of volunteerism have been firmly planted not just in the United States but around the world. But there is much more to do. Service organizations in developing countries offer many opportunities for people who want to help construct a building or work on a social-service project. Hospitals and nursing-care facilities are always looking for volunteers. Mentoring organizations such as Big Brothers Big Sisters need more mature adults who can offer not money but quality time, wisdom, and guidance to those in their formative years. Children—especially those with special needs—are waiting in line to be adopted by loving parents. Anyone with the desire to become more generous with his or her time and talents should have no trouble finding an opportunity.

Affirming Human Dignity

Millard Fuller, founder of the international home-building organization Habitat for Humanity, tells the story of a neighborhood

To welcome the weeping widow;
to provide for her a place to rest; to dry up her tears;
to feed and educate her little orphans,
and to put them in a way to gain an honest livelihood.
To take by the hand poor young tradesmen;
to lend them money; to set them up, and thus
to ennoble them to be very useful to the community,
and to make comfortable livings for themselves.

—BENJAMIN FRANKLIN

work project in which former President Jimmy Carter partici-
pated. A year or so after the work was completed, Fuller returned
for a visit. A young boy came out of the house to greet him. Fuller
recognized that the boy had come out of the very house that
Jimmy Carter had worked on.

"Hey," he said, "you got a pretty car."

"Yes, and you have a pretty house. Which one
is yours?"

He waved a finger back toward the house.

"What's your name?" Millard asked him.

"D.J."

"Well, D.J., I want to ask you a question. Who built
your house?"

Millard thought he would say, "Jimmy Carter."
Instead, he quietly replied, "Jesus."

Jesus built his house. He knew. A mere lad, he had
gotten the message.

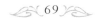

One man gives freely, yet gains evermore;
another withholds unduly, but comes to poverty.
A generous man will prosper;
he who refreshes others will himself be refreshed.

—**PROVERBS 11:24–25**

One of the distinctions of Habitat for Humanity is that it encourages those who are being helped to participate in the effort so that they will have a sense of control and ownership, thus enabling them to claim their dignity as human beings. This approach, in fact, serves as an effective model of thrift and generosity by enabling individuals to work toward becoming self-sufficient (thrift) and by demonstrating selfless generosity that is no longer necessary when the task is completed.

We mentioned above Maimonides' penultimate level of charity. The ultimate level, he taught, consisted of giving people jobs or no-interest loans so they could adequately support themselves and not need charity. Generosity that affirms the humanity of others by allowing them to become self-sufficient is genuine. So-called generosity that confines people to positions of need is shortsighted and perhaps selfish. True generosity rids itself of the need to be needed, just as truly loving parents teach their children to become self-sufficient, even though this entails risking that those same children will abandon their parents once they no longer need them.

Various recent surveys and polls suggest that when it comes to generosity, we have a long way to go as a society. This is true even among those who take religion most seriously. According to one poll, only 8 percent of those who call themselves "born again" give at least 10 percent of their earnings to churches or charities. Another poll revealed that 77 percent of evangelicals say that volunteer service is "very important," but only 32 percent actually volunteer "a lot."

I dream of a world where generosity becomes an essential value—a routine part of life—of a world where giving to others is regarded as a welcomed opportunity, not a burdensome obligation. It is useful to think how blessed we would be if we experienced an epidemic of generosity in our country and in our world. As we shall soon see, this could very well result in an epidemic of joy.

· THE RELATIONSHIP BETWEEN
THRIFT AND GENEROSITY ·

In the first section of this book, we explored thrift, contending that a commitment to thrift—complete with the kinds of attitudes and behaviors that such a commitment produces—is inherently virtuous. This is the case because the discipline of thrift is ennobling in and of itself. But even more uplifting is an adherence to thrifty living as a means to pursue some larger goal or advance some greater virtue.

Some embark on lives of thrift for mostly self-serving reasons. They work hard and make good decisions. They spend wisely, invest wisely, and have the discipline to live well within their means. But the whole goal of their thrifty living is to ensure that 1) they will have more to spend later on, and 2) they will never run out of resources. They are experts at delaying gratification, but are ultimately unwilling to limit the gratification they have earned and feel they have coming.

As inherently virtuous as thrifty living is, its capacity to influence the world for good is severely limited if its goals are ultimately merely self-serving ones. In contrast, the potential for good is greatly magnified when the virtue of thrift is combined not with selfishness, but with the virtue of generosity.

As he formed his perspectives on philanthropy, my father came to recognize that philanthropy can and should serve as a catalyst to help others in time to become producers and givers. Such thinking incorporates an element of thrift in the pursuit of philanthropy: The more people are willing and able to be generous, the more good can be accomplished.

Thrift for a Noble Purpose

Among the distinctions of the Templeton Foundation is its emphasis on finding and pursuing a noble purpose in life. William

Damon explored this concept in his 2003 book, *Noble Purpose: The Joy of Living a Meaningful Life*, published by Templeton Foundation Press. It is hard for me to imagine a greater, nobler purpose than to combine a life of thrift with a commitment to generosity. Imagine people who are industrious, creative, hard-working, frugal, wise, trustworthy, and disciplined. All these qualities influence how they manage resources of time, talent, and money. The goal, however, is not to serve themselves, but to make life better for others in ways that elevate their dignity and self-respect.

This ideal—this challenge to combine thrift and generosity—is certainly present within my Christian religious tradition. Jesus admonished his followers, "Do not store up for yourselves treasures on earth, where moth and rust destroy, and where thieves break in and steal. But store up for yourselves treasures in heaven, where moth and rust do not destroy, and where thieves do not break in and steal." I believe we store up treasures in heaven by

Don't give until it hurts. Give until it feels good.

—CLIFF JONES

———— • ————

No one can serve two masters.
Either he will hate the one and love the other,
or he will be devoted to one and despise the other.
You cannot serve both God and money.

—MATTHEW 6:24

following Jesus' example of caring for those among us who are most vulnerable, those most in need of help, by providing a "hand-up" in a way that most upholds the dignity of the recipient.

The Apostle Paul certainly understood the concept of combining thrift and generosity. In his *Freedom of Simplicity,* Richard Foster observes that in Paul's letter to the Ephesians, Paul contends that "the reason to acquire money was not to build a nest egg but to help people in need."

THRIFT, GENEROSITY, AND THE PURSUIT OF HAPPINESS

If you ask people what they want out of life, most will respond predictably by saying that all they want is to be happy. They want happiness for themselves, for their children, and for other loved ones. As noted earlier, in our nation's Declaration of Independence, "the pursuit of happiness" is stressed as one of the fundamental goals of our nation's founders. For a great many people, this goal remains intact over two and a quarter centuries later.

Regarding happiness, the comedian Henny Youngman once quipped, "What good is happiness? It can't buy money." Much truth is spoken in this jest; namely, for many people, happiness is inconceivable apart from material wealth.

Most will state for the record that money can't buy happiness. It's what we've been trained to say; and it's what religious leaders have told us we should believe. But if people truly believe this, how do we explain the long lines that form at quick-shop markets every time the lottery jackpot goes over $100 million? The truth is, many if not most people don't practice what they preach when it comes to the relationship between money and happiness.

A quip in Richard Foster's *Freedom of Simplicity* attributed to the late John D. Rockefeller more truly represents the majority's perspective on money. Rockefeller was asked how much money it would take for him to be totally satisfied. His response: "Just a little bit more."

Fortunately, there is reason to believe and to hope that our culture's perspectives on money and happiness may soon be undergoing a revolution. The body of research into what makes people happy is relatively new and small, but the preliminary results unequivocally support what religious teachers have been saying all along: that money really *can't* buy happiness. In fact, the studies indicate that a preoccupation with material possessions can actually prevent us from attaining the very happiness money is supposed to produce.

In his book *The Progress Paradox*, Gregg Easterbrook summarizes the results of the research most plainly: "The percentage of Americans who describe themselves as 'happy' has not budged since the 1950s, though the typical person's real income doubled during that period." He adds, "Far from feeling better about their lives, many are feeling worse. Throughout the United States and the European Union, incidence of clinical melancholy has been rising in eerie synchronization with rising prosperity."

You cannot be lonely if you help the lonely.

—SIR JOHN TEMPLETON

———— • ————

There is a wonderful law of nature
that the three things we crave the most in life—
happiness, freedom, and peace of mind—
are always obtained
by giving them to someone else.

—PAYTON MARCH

To be sure, at some income levels, the research reveals a positive correlation between happiness and material resources. Specifically, people who struggle to fulfill their basic human needs—food, shelter, rest, social contact, and at least some leisure time—are clearly not as happy as those who don't have to worry about going hungry or having a roof over their heads. But once we get beyond life's necessities, the correlation between income and happiness is, in the words of University of Michigan researcher Ronald Inglehart, "surprisingly weak." Inglehart reached this conclusion in 1990 based on a study of 170,000 people in sixteen nations.

For those who have reflected on the times when they have felt most content, most happy, perhaps this "surprisingly weak" connection between money and happiness should not be so surprising. In our medical careers, the greatest happiness for my wife, Pina, and me came from interceding in some child's life in a way that preserved his or her life and/or enhanced his or her quality of life and potential to make a contribution in life. In that regard, I recall another one of my father's favorite laws of life—that happiness should not be a goal, but that "happiness is always a by-product."

I am sure that many other people have not experienced the happiest, most joyful times in their lives during an expensive vacation or cruise. Perhaps they felt happiest and most joyful at a yearly family reunion picnic, during a hike in the woods, or in midnight conversations around a summer campfire, all of which come with a negligible price tag. For my wife and me, our best times were the births of our children and grandchildren. I know for a fact that people who come together to help other people in need often experience a kind of deep-seated joy and contentment that no Caribbean cruise—no matter how elaborate and pricey—could ever come close to matching. As Barbara Hansen, a paraplegic for many years, writes: "We won't find joy 'out there'; it comes from within. It rests on an inner strength that endures despite life's ups and downs, an inner strength found only by knowing what really matters." What really matters is also acknowledged by an ancient Chinese proverb: "One joy scatters a hundred griefs."

LEARNING TO BE SATISFIED

David G. Myers of Hope College, author of several books, including *The Pursuit of Happiness: Who Is Happy and Why,* is widely and deservedly credited with both originating and publicizing much of the research pertaining to money and happiness. He observes, "Happiness seems less a matter of getting what we want than of wanting what we have."

Contentment or joy, then, is a higher level of fulfillment than happiness. Far more than material goals, our goals of touching lives in a meaningful way, of striving to leave things better than we found them—these are goals that are much more likely to provide joy and fulfillment as by-products. As the philosopher Seneca put it, "No one can be poor who has enough,

Money never stays with me. It would burn me if it did.
I throw it out of my hands as soon as possible,
lest it should find its way within my heart.

—JOHN WESLEY

———•———

The real duty of man is not to extend his power
or multiply his wealth beyond his needs,
but to enrich and enjoy
his imperishable possession: his soul.

—GILBERT HIGHET

nor rich who covets more." Perhaps this explains why, according to Myers, paralyzed persons report being happier than lottery winners. Someone who cannot walk has learned to modify his or her expectations and aim for things that matter, whereas lottery winners learn the hard way that money cannot deliver on its utopian-sounding promises.

Unfortunately, we have been conditioned by Madison Avenue to believe that we must have the newest car, the biggest television, and the most impressive jewelry. So long as what a person wants is always and inevitably more, that person ultimately can never be satisfied.

According to Gregg Easterbrook, "Seeking to placate the pang of want through acquisition can become like habituation to a drug—you need to keep buying more and more to get the same high, and the high wears off faster all the time."

David Myers discusses this dynamic by invoking what he calls the principle of adaptation. He states, "Once adapted to a new level of affluence, it takes a higher high to rejuice the joy. I can recall the thrill of watching my family's 12-inch, black-and-white television set. Now, if the color goes out on our 25-inch TV, I feel deprived. Having adapted upward, I perceive as negative what I once experienced as positive."

Our hunger for more can turn into a vicious cycle. The more "material" we have, the more we want, and vice versa. But fortunately, adaptation applies in both directions: upward and downward. We can adapt downward by choosing not to seek the luxuries we have too easily taken for granted. How ironic and fascinating that we can increase our capacity for truly enjoying and appreciating the good things in life by denying ourselves from time to time instead of by engaging in them incessantly. But it is true. Even common foods light up our taste buds after a period of fasting. As Ben Franklin put it, "Hunger is the best pickle."

Money as a Barrier to Happiness

A man attended a soccer game one afternoon to see his daughter play. He had to park his brand new Lexus a hundred yards or so from the field. Shortly after the game started, he noticed some teenagers milling about the parking lot. He missed his daughter's goal because he ended up spending the afternoon babysitting his new car, so concerned was he that something might happen to it. This man didn't own the Lexus—the Lexus owned him.

To repeat, money can be freeing when used wisely and when we see ourselves as stewards of our resources and not as covetous owners. But if we allow our possessions to capture our hearts and minds, then they will eventually enslave us. The more we have, the more we have to manage and to fret over.

The *Philadelphia Inquirer* ran an article on Jack Whittaker on the first anniversary of his winning the highest undivided jackpot in lottery history, over $300 million. The article pointed out that security guards now had to watch over his home and

Think of the misery that comes into our lives
by our restless gnawing greed.
We plunge ourselves into enormous debt
and then take two and three jobs to stay afloat.
We uproot our families with unnecessary moves
just so we can have a more prestigious house.
We grasp and grab and never have enough.

—RICHARD FOSTER

office. Whittaker lamented that his granddaughter had lost all her friends. "They want her for her money and not for her good personality," he said. "She's the most bitter 16-year-old I know." How sad to see a presumably nice young woman's life made miserable not by poverty, but by wealth. The lives of the Whittaker family would be so different if they looked at their sudden wealth with the hearts and minds of stewards, if they sought God's will and guidance in nurturing their resources in a way that did not enslave them but instead optimized their abilities to make a meaningful impact as givers.

For the people of ancient Israel, there was a remedy to this slavery to wealth: the Year of Jubilee; in effect, a leveling of the playing field every fifty years. By and large, when commentators discuss the Jubilee principle, found in the book of Leviticus, they view it in terms of a redistribution of wealth or an equitable reordering of social structures. If we focus only on this aspect, however, we fail to recognize that there is also something to be

gained by those who are giving away power, land, or wealth. Foster views the Jubilee principle in part as "a call to divinely enabled freedom from possessions." In other words, one of its purposes was to break the addiction to "more" that diverts us from putting God first in our lives and from the joy that God intends for us.

I dream of a time when people want to gain from their own labor—from what they earn—not by getting something for nothing. I also dream of a time when the goal of such hard-earned gains is focused on others. Then joy will flow both from the dignity of hard work, savings, and thrift, as well as from the sense of meaning and purpose in a life committed to putting God and others before yourself.

Joy and the Search for Community

David Myers says it well: "More than ever, we have big houses and broken homes, high incomes and low morale, secured rights and diminished civility. We excel at making a living but often fail at making a life. We celebrate our prosperity but yearn for purpose. We cherish our freedoms but long for connection. In an age of plenty, we feel spiritual hunger."

Indeed, we do long for connection, for friendship, for close meaningful relationships with other people. In *Bird by Bird*, Anne Lamott writes that when you have a great friend, who holds your attention and makes you laugh,

> she can say, "Hey, I've got to drive up to the dump in Petaluma—wanna come along?" and you honestly can't think of anything in the world you'd rather do. By the same token, a boring or annoying person can offer to buy you an expensive dinner, followed by tickets for a great show, and in all honesty you'd rather stay at home and watch the aspic set.

We long for community, meaning, and purpose. Indeed, human beings were created to live in community, especially in a community that manifests an altruistic spirit of giving to others. That

There are two ways to get enough:
one is to continue to accumulate more and more.
The other is to desire less.

—G. K. CHESTERTON

———— • ————

Giving friendship is more important
than giving luxuries.

—SIR JOHN TEMPLETON

is why solitary confinement is a prison within a prison. Being in the presence of others, even if they are thieves and robbers, is preferable to being alone. Granted, there are times when we need or desire solitude, but some of life's greatest joys are experienced in the company of others.

When we exercise the virtue of generosity, we create and experience the joy of community. This dynamic is part of our tradition as a nation. When Alexis de Tocqueville came to America in 1831, he was impressed among other things by what he described as a pervasive spirit of service and volunteerism. This spirit, de Tocqueville maintained, helped to ameliorate the potential tension between the rule of the majority and the rights of the minority. In essence, people did not depend on the government to provide what they needed. They helped one another.

This positive philanthropic spirit is perhaps best exemplified by the rural American tradition of barn raising. If a family in the community needed a barn, it was not just their problem—

it was everyone's problem. It was also everyone's opportunity to help. When we share with others—and receive what others have to share with us—we experience the joy that comes from being a part of a community.

I fear that in our modern world we have lost sight of what it means to be in relation to others. We have forgotten the benefits of living in community. Gone are the front porches where people would stop by and not just exchange pleasantries but also share both needs and offers of help. In many places, isolated, monolithic, gated communities have replaced neighborhoods where people of various social classes used to mingle. Computer entertainment has replaced pick-up baseball games. People keep to themselves.

We cannot fight modernity; we cannot turn back time. Community bowling leagues and tug-of-war matches at church picnics may be less common. We can, however, find ways to counteract the negative effects of our culture's overemphasis on living for one's self—what some call "radical personal autonomy." One way to do this is by making a concerted effort to become more involved in the lives of others by being more generous with our time and our material resources. Such an effort, I believe, holds the key to rediscovering the joy of living as we have been created to live: in community with others and with the God who continues to bless us in so many different ways.

Peace That Passes Understanding

I heard recently about a man who was suffering from mild depression. He couldn't quite pinpoint why. Nothing in his life had changed. Nothing bad had happened. But nothing good had happened, either. He was in a rut. This man went to his boss, with whom he had a very good relationship. After listening to his employee, the boss, without hesitating, suggested that his friend spend the following Saturday volunteering at a soup kitchen. The boss provided a phone number and an address, and the man took his advice.

When sailing on the Titanic,
even first class cannot get you
where you want to go.

—DAVID MYERS

———— • ————

Happiness makes up in height
what it lacks in length.

—ROBERT FROST

Sure enough, the plan worked. Something about helping other people who needed a little help gave this man a sense of purpose that brought his energy back. He tasted a bit of the joy that comes from serving others.

My father conveys a similar testimony in the book *Worldwide Laws of Life*. A man who had been dishonorably discharged after eighteen years in the military found himself on the streets with little hope for his future. While waiting in a soup line at a church-run center one day, he responded to a request for volunteers to help someone move furniture. It was the first time he had done anything for someone other than himself for a long time. And it felt good!

So he kept volunteering. He volunteered as a typist at the center, and soon this turned into a job. He moved off the streets and began renting a room from one of his coworkers. He went on to manage a community food closet and was able to rent his own apartment. In short, giving to others turned his life around.

In this same book, my father suggests several maxims that address this theme: "By giving you grow"; "It is better to love than to be loved" (Saint Francis of Assisi); "The only way to have a friend is to be a friend" (Ralph Waldo Emerson); "Love conquers all things" (Virgil); "You are sought after if you reflect love, joy, peace, patience, kindness, goodness, faithfulness, gentleness, and self-control."

These stories and many more that could be told convince me that joy and spiritual contentment can be found in their greatest measure by combining the virtues of thrift and generosity. Can it be a spiritual law of the universe that we find joy and happiness by bringing joy and happiness to others? Can it be that the more thrifty and generous we are, the more we will experience the joy and peace that pass understanding?

I believe with Barbara Hansen that Father John Powell is right in his assessment: The kind of love that brings joy into our lives is the love that shows "concern for the satisfaction, security, and development of the one loved."

John Wesley, the founder of Methodism, advocated the combined virtues of thrift and generosity when he said, "Make all you can, save all you can, give all you can." We can all pursue this goal, no matter how much or how little we have.

Sophie was a young immigrant from Germany who struggled with the English language. The only work she could find was scrubbing floors in the office buildings of Lower Manhattan. Every night from 10 p.m. until 6 a.m. she scrubbed floors, emptied trash, and dusted furniture. When she was young, she had a burning desire to become a missionary to Africa. But she lacked the education and the resources to do so. And over the years, rheumatism began to take over her body.

But early on, Sophie had learned the blessings of tithing. She began putting away one-tenth of her income to support a missionary to Africa in her stead. By the end of her life, she

*[T]hose persons who are on
the leading edge of evolution realize . . .
that the greatest happiness in life comes,
not from the comforts and pleasures
that money can buy,
but from the investment of the days
of our lives in a purpose which transcends
our purely personal interests.*

— SIR JOHN TEMPLETON

was able to provide for not just one representative to the mission field of Africa, but six! All on a so-called scrubwoman's salary.

My father has said that one of his major regrets in life was not beginning his mutual funds earlier, because had he done so, he would have been able to help even more people than he did. Nevertheless, later in life, my father decided that he had at least made a useful contribution of over fifty years in trying to contribute to people's material wealth. Then, at age eighty-two, he retired from investment management of other people's financial assets. He did so because he wished instead to devote the rest of his life to help people prosper even more wonderfully by encouraging investments in spiritual wealth. In this way, he could empower and ennoble the lives of many more people than he had been able to help with their financial investments.

In his lifetime of learning what really matters in life, my father said that one of his discoveries is that "happiness comes

*Learning to be satisfied with what we have
rather than desiring more, more, more—
this is the essence of joy.*

—BARBARA HANSEN

———— • ————

*Love cures people: the ones who receive love
and the ones who give it, too.*

—DR. KARL A. MENNINGER

from spiritual wealth, not material wealth." It was from my father that I also learned about the blessings of thrift and generosity—especially when they are coupled together. In that regard, he shared with me the understanding that "joy is not in things, but is in you."

In conclusion, I hope this book is a beginning for you and not an ending. I invite you to learn more about thrift and generosity, to embrace these virtues, to make them more and more a part of your life as you strive to discover a greater sense of meaning and purpose. I believe that as you combine the virtues of thrift and generosity—thus bringing comfort, healing, hope, kindness, happiness, and love into the lives of others—you, as have many others, will discover deep and unanticipated wells of joy along the way.

· RECOMMENDED READING ·

Damon, William. 2003. *Noble Purpose: The Joy of Living a Meaningful Life.* Philadelphia, Penna.: Templeton Foundation Press.

Easterbrook, Gregg. 2003. *The Progress Paradox: How Life Gets Better While People Feel Worse.* New York, N.Y.: Random House.

Foster, Richard J. 1981. *Freedom of Simplicity.* New York, N.Y.: HarperCollins.

Fuller, Millard and Linda Fuller. 1990. *The Excitement Is Building: How Habitat for Humanity Is Putting Roofs over Heads and Hope in Hearts.* Nashville, Tenn.: W Publishing Group.

Kasser, Tim. 2002. *The High Price of Materialism.* Cambridge, Mass.: The MIT Press.

Longacre, Doris Janzen. 1980. *Living More with Less.* Scottdale, Penna.: Herald Press.

Moore, Gary. 1997. *Spiritual Investments: Wall Street Wisdom from the Career of Sir John Templeton.* Philadelphia, Penna.: Templeton Foundation Press.

Noll, Mark A. 2001. *God and Mammon: Protestants, Money, and the Market,* 1790-1860. Oxford: Oxford University Press.

Schneider, John. 1994. *Godly Materialism: Rethinking Money & Possessions.* Downers Grove, Ill.: InterVarsity Press.

———. 2002. *The Good of Affluence: Seeking God in a Culture of Wealth.* Grand Rapids, Mich.: William B. Eerdmans Publishing Company.

Sider, Ronald J. 1997. *Rich Christians in an Age of Hunger: Moving from Affluence to Generosity (20th Anniversary Revision).* Nashville, Tenn.: W Publishing Group.

Templeton, John Marks. 1997. *Worldwide Laws of Life: 200 Eternal Spiritual Principles.* Philadelphia, Penna.: Templeton Foundation Press.

———. 2002. *Wisdom from World Religions: Pathways toward Heaven on Earth.* Philadelphia, Penna.: Templeton Foundation Press.

Wheeler, Sondra Ely. 1995. *Wealth As Peril and Obligation: The New Testament on Possessions.* Grand Rapids, Mich.: William B. Eerdmans Publishing Company.